Learning To Say *No*
Without Feeling Guilty

by
Roberts Liardon

HARRISON HOUSE
Tulsa, Oklahoma

7th Printing
Over 42,000 in Print

Learning To Say No
Without Feeling Guilty
ISBN 0-89274-537-1
Copyright © 1988 by
Roberts Liardon Ministries
P. O. Box 30710
Laguna Hills, CA 92654

Published by Harrison House, Inc.
P O. Box 35035
Tulsa, Oklahoma 74153

CONTENTS

1
Saying No

The world has discovered a valuable word: *No*. The secular media have made *no* a household word by popularizing the "Just Say No" drug campaign. That slogan is being advertised on television, radio, and billboards, and in magazines and newspapers. Finally, the world has realized the importance of saying *no* to some things.

However, it is time the Church of Jesus Christ rediscovered this very important, priceless word, this little but very powerful word. After all, God was the first to advocate the concept for which the word stands: denying Satan, denying the bondage others seek to hold you in, and denying self.

Every preacher and every lay person needs to learn to say *no*. In fact, every human being needs to learn to say *no*.

Undoubtedly everyone has been in a situation where he wished he had said *no* instead of *yes*. However, because he had given his word, he went ahead and did whatever was involved. He kept his "contract." Perhaps saying *yes* not only led to inconvenience but to sin. He did not sin by breaking his word, but he sinned by grumbling and complaining or by criticizing and finding fault. Perhaps he sinned by getting into resentment and bitterness, or even unforgiveness toward the other person or people involved.

Many people seem to be afraid to say *no*. They seem to equate *no* with negative things and with having no fun or joy in life. Nothing could be farther from the truth.

The Bible says, **Restore unto me the *joy* of thy salvation . . .** (Ps. 51:12).

Check Your Joy and Peace Gauges

Christians should have joy, vitality, and fun in what they are doing. If there is no joy, something is very wrong. There is joy in God's presence, and if you are doing what is right (His will), you are in His presence, and He is in your presence.

Every now and then we need to check up on our joy and peace gauges as we drive down the road called "Life." If those gauges are on empty, we need to get refilled. We should not let our joy and peace run low any more than the gasoline in our vehicles.

Phyllis Mackall of Tulsa, Oklahoma, is not only a member of my board of directors, but a precious friend. The daughter of a Pentecostal minister, she is very knowledgeable about Pentecostal history. In addition, she has wisdom. When she talks, I listen.

Once she told me, "There are two things every person in the ministry needs to learn to say: *No* and *Thank you.*"

Her advice was both wise and true. If we say *yes* when it should have been *no*, we get into trouble, and when we forget to show appreciation to people, we cause trouble and hurt. Everyone needs to say *no* and *thank you* more often.

How often have you said *no* and gotten into trouble? Usually, more trouble comes from saying *yes*. We need to learn to say *no* without feeling guilty about it. Sometimes *no* is God's anointed answer for a situation.

If you begin saying *no*, soon you will know how to say it and smile. *No* is a wonderful word. Phyllis helped me learn the value of that little, powerful word.

I would go over to her house, and she would say, "Roberts, what's the anointed word?"

I would say, "*No.*"

And she would say, "That's not loud enough. That's not strong enough. You don't believe it quite yet. Say it again."

She would have me say it over and over until it came out loud, strong, and bold.

"That's it. You've got it," she would finally say.

Sometimes you have to yell something to make every part of you hear it. If you speak softly, what you say seems to carry no weight even with your own self. Learn to say *no* boldly.

Let's look at the first example in the Bible of people who said *yes* when they should have said *no* and suffered serious consequences. God has never been afraid of *no*. That word is used in the Bible over and over again from Genesis to Revelation.

2

The First No

God told Adam and Eve, "You can eat from any tree except one."

"*No*," God said, "you may not eat of this one tree."

We all know what happened when they disobeyed God's *no*. Was God being mean? Certainly not. His prohibition was for their own protection. *No* is often a word of protection for your personal life, your family, your business, your church, and your nation.

God has His children's best interests in mind when He says *no*. Then the serpent came along and tried to turn God's *no* into a *yes*. He told Eve the fruit was good for her because it would make her just like God.

Instead of yelling *no* at the devil, Eve began to think, "Well, that fruit does look good. God could not have *really* meant for us not to eat of it."

Yes, He did. When God says *no*, He means *no*. When He says *yes*, He means *yes*. But Eve ate of the fruit and gave some to Adam, who then had his chance to say *no* and turn things around. But Adam put Eve before God and joined her in eating the fruit. The consequence was that both lost everything.

If Adam and Eve had obeyed God's first *no*, they would still be in the Garden of Eden, eating, having fun, and enjoying life. They could have continued to live in perfect joy, but they lost everything.

When you allow your mind to be enticed by what is not the will of God, you will soon act on that enticement. What you think about, you will soon do. Adam ate the fruit and was miserable — the state of all those who say *yes* when they should have said *no*.

Success is not built on how many times you say *yes*. Usually, success is built on how many times you say a strong *no* — and stick to it. A weak *no* too easily can be turned into a *yes*.

No **Runs From the Appearance of Evil**

No has legs. It is a force that runs from the appearance of evil. Those who say *no* do not walk with the ungodly, stand with sinners, nor sit with those who are scornful of God's ways. (Ps. 1:1.) *No* never stays in a place where evil abounds.

No has actions and a big voice. The Bible says if we do not do what we know to do, we have sinned. (James 4:17.) Not saying *no* when we know to do so is sin.

Often, *no* is very hard to say, but once you have said it, you will feel like a giant. You will be happy and proud of yourself. *No* stops conflicts of doubt and guilt. *No* has no suspicion in it.

No is a universal word: it is known all over the world. Even where people do not speak English, they know what *no* means — which can be very important when you are traveling abroad!

3

Say *No* to the Flesh

Let's look at another Biblical example: Samson. (Judges 16.)

Samson was mightily used of God. When the anointing came on him, he had strength no one else had. He could easily get the best of the Philistines. He was so strong that he could do nearly anything he wanted to do. He was respected by everyone, greatly esteemed by the leaders of Israel, and feared by the leaders of the Philistines.

He had a big problem, however. He would not say *no* to his flesh. He liked beautiful women, and the sad thing is that he preferred pagan women. Probably, he could have had any marriageable girl he wanted from among the Israelites, but he only wanted foreign women.

He said to his father, "Go over there to that other nation and get that woman for me."

His parents asked, "What is wrong with you? Why can you not find a girl among our own people whom you would like to have as your wife?"

Then Samson threw a tantrum. Flesh always has tantrums, just as a child does.

If you are a parent who knows how to say *no* and keep your word, you can look at a child having a tantrum and say, "Now that is enough! Stop that right now," and your child will stop.

But Samson's father did not do that. He gave in to his son's demands.

First of all, Samson should have said *no* to himself. Before you can say *no* to anyone else, you have to learn to say it to yourself. Before you can look someone else straight in the eye, say *no*, and not feel guilty about it, you must learn to deny your own mind and your own flesh. Then it becomes a lot easier to say *no* to others.

Also, you need to remember this: Silence usually means *yes* in people's minds. You need to verbalize your stand.

Learn to make your body walk the bedroom floor and pray, even when it rises up and screams, "I want to sleep."

Or your mind may say, "What do you think you are doing? You do not have time to pray now. You have to do the laundry, remember?" (Or wash the car, or call someone you have not talked to in six years.)

Say, "No, I am going to pray in tongues for an hour and enjoy every minute of it." Then do it.

4

No Is Not Maybe

No is a spiritual word, and spiritual words are absolutes. There is no "maybe" and no wondering in the realm of the Spirit. Most people do not like that, however. If you stand on your "yeas" and your "nays" (Matt. 5:37), they will say you are into spiritual pride. The world basically is very wishy-washy, but the Church should not be following the same path. We need to say *no* a lot stronger than we have been saying it.

There is no neutrality in the spiritual world, no "summit meetings" in order to find a compromise. Heaven and Hell are white and black. There is no gray, no lukewarmness. Jesus said to be hot or cold, or He would spew you out of His mouth. (Rev. 3:15,16.) His words are absolutes, and our words need to become absolute again. Words are important.

Saying *yes* to Delilah did not stop with the sin of cohabiting with a pagan woman. It led to dire consequences for Samson and for Israel.

She began to ask Samson, "Where does your strength come from?"

Instead of saying, "No. I am not going to tell you, so don't ever ask me again," Samson tried to put her off with jokes and then lies. But she would not be put off.

"If you love me, you'll tell me. You are making a fool out of me," she said.

The Bible relates that she kept pressing him daily so that his soul was vexed. In other words, she kept nagging him until he did not know what was right and what was wrong. Finally, he gave in and told her what she wanted to know, although he knew that was wrong.

Samson would not say *no* to himself or to Delilah. He woke up one morning with his eyes poked out and spent the rest of his life like a donkey grinding meal. Even though his death was a final triumph, his life was shortened and his work for the Lord defeated.

"Delilahs" Are Around Today

Some people want explanations for your *no* so they can find a way to trick you by your own words. They are "Delilahs" who search for a crack into the door of your words in order to cause your *no* to become a *yes*.

People like that are sly as a snake. They slither in and poke their heads in places they have no business being. Then you are surprised they got there.

When you say *no*, the windows will crash down, the blinds will be drawn, and the doors will slam shut and lock. If you are strong in your answer and do not waver, no one can slither in and change your mind. They might pound and knock, but they cannot get in, because *no* has been declared. When it is spoken with spiritual force, it cannot be penetrated.

In this hour, we are going through the greatest war the Church has ever had in the natural and in the spiritual realms. A lot of the battles do not have to exist, if we will just make a bold proclamation to the evil spirits: *No*, you cannot come in here. *No*, you cannot do that. *No* . . . period. That will stop unnecessary battles.

Say *no* more often, and you will not have to pray a half-million words trying to get victory. Say *no*, decree it, and stand on it. *No* is a wonderful word. It is too bad Samson did not know how wonderful it is. He did not fulfill his destiny because he would not say *no*. If you do not say *no* to yourself, you will not say *no* to the "Delilahs."

5

No Cannot Always Be Nice

King Saul was another person who did not value this little two-letter word as he should have.

> **Then came the word of the Lord unto Samuel, saying,**
>
> **It repenteth me that I have set up Saul to be king: for he is turned back from following me, and hath not performed my commandments. And it grieved Samuel; and he cried unto the Lord all night.**
>
> **1 Samuel 15:10,11**

Verses 13 through 21 tell us that Samuel came to Saul and asked, "Have you done what God commanded?"

Saul lied, "I have done all the Lord has commanded."

Then Samuel said, "What is the bleating of the sheep and the lowing of the oxen that I hear?"

He confronted Saul, "Stop, and let me tell you what the Lord told me tonight."

But when Saul was confronted, he blamed the people. Sounds like Adam again, doesn't it? Or perhaps like Aaron excusing himself for not telling the people *no* when they wanted a golden calf. (Ex. 32:22-24.)

Saul told Samuel the people had made him keep back some of the choice animals from slaughter in order

17

to sacrifice them to God. That was so ridiculous. Saul was the king, and people then had to obey the king.

If you pleased the king, you would be happy for a very good reason: The king would not chop your head off! You would have great favor by making the king happy. There was power in the words of a king. All Saul had to do was say *no* to the people, but he feared their opinion of him, and he let his *no* become a *yes*.

Saul probably thought, "Samuel's not being reasonable here. I will be nice to the people."

Being Nice May Cost You

Being nice cost Saul dearly, and it cost the people dearly. It cost him not only his throne but his life and the lives of his sons!

You cannot live in a place of compromise or neutrality with God. You are either all the way in, or you are not in at all. Without God's absolutes we will never walk in the realm of the Spirit. We must learn to say *no* to the desires of the flesh, to the world, to the devil, and to other people who would lead us away from God and His ways.

We should learn from the examples in the Bible. The mistakes made by Biblical leaders are written down for our example and can save us hours of heartache. The word *no* can especially save pastors hours of heartache.

How many times has a pastor said *yes* to someone and allowed him to preach from his pulpit knowing he should have said *no*? Then it takes him hours to undo what one man does in five minutes from the pulpit — all because the pastor did not want to hurt someone's feelings. For lack of a *no*, the sheep were exposed to error, division, or false spirits.

I have been in some churches where people have said to the pastor, "We want to come to your church."

The pastor had agreed, although he knew those people would not be good members — and they destroyed the church. He did not want to hurt their feelings, but a church split hurt worse and hurt more people than saying *no* in the beginning would have.

Basically, all of us want to be nice, and we want everyone to like us. We must love everyone, but we do not have to accept all that comes with everyone. God loves the world but hates sin. He accepts the sinner but rejects the sin.

6

Power, Not Politics

Christians must make a decision: Are they going to be political or powerful?

God is powerful, but He is not political. Politics is false power. Religious politics is one of the major traps ministries need to avoid. Religious politics gives people a false sense of power and influence.

If you "play politics," you may think you have influence, but it will not last. The person who put you in position can pull the rug out from under you and stop you from giving out the word of the Lord. Do not be political. Just be powerful in the Lord.

Politicians rarely, if ever, use *no* or *yes*. Instead, they say, "Let's discuss it." In religious politics as well, there is never a right or a wrong. There is only whoever is the strongest or whoever has the most power and money. People who go the route of religious politics do and say things simply to please others, usually to gain something. That is why they do not like Christians who move in the prophetic flow of the Lord.

Prophets or those who operate prophetically stand on the Word of God and say, "This is truth. This is the absolute standard. What you are saying or doing is wrong."

Those rebuked many times will reply, "How do you know? You are in pride."

Truth is truth. When you agree with it, you are right. When you disagree, you are wrong. When I preach the Word of God, I am right. If I preach personal convictions, I could be wrong. When I preach chapter and verse, it is right, and I do not have to apologize for it. I do not have to withdraw and consider what people are going to think of me. As long as I preach the truth, God will give me success. It is the same for anyone else. Preach the truth, and do not waver.

God Does Not Accept *Maybe*

God has a *yes* and a *no*. When you stand before Him, you are either saved or you are not. You will not be able to get away with a *maybe*. You will not be able to figure how many good deeds equal a *yes*. Accepting Jesus is the only way to salvation. If you are not saved, it does not matter how many services you have been to or how many good deeds you have done.

Some people say, "You are too harsh. That scares people. That offends people."

I would rather tell people the truth and risk offending them, than not tell the truth and be responsible for them going to Hell through misunderstanding what I meant. If it is not *yes* with Heaven, they are going to Hell. Some people blush at the word *Hell*. There is a Hell, and there is a Heaven, and there is *no* in-between. There is no neutrality with God.

Political spirits do not like "*yes* or *no*" people. When people who take strong stands meet political people, there is usually a battle. Political people always want to have a "summit meeting" to discuss ideas, opinions, and so on. They say they want a neutral balance, when all they really want is for you to compromise and agree with them. You cannot balance the truth. Truth already is as balanced as it is ever going to be.

7

Grounds for
True Fellowship

There is a strong movement today toward church unity. Part of that movement is of God, but part of it is not. What are the grounds for Christian fellowship? What is true Christian fellowship?

I see three ingredients that are necessary for true fellowship:

(1) Those in agreement must respect one another.

(2) They must believe the same things.

(3) They must have the same desires for the Kingdom.

If you do not respect someone else, you cannot really fellowship with him. Without equal respect for one another's integrity and spiritual strength, imbalance results.

Also, it is not true fellowship unless both parties believe the same things. Otherwise, it will be a false unity, and conflict will result sooner or later.

True Christian fellowship means you have the same desires for the Kingdom. Some people are not concerned with furthering God's Kingdom on earth at all. Some want to establish their own little kingdoms. They may say they are in the ministry for God's Kingdom, but they really are not. Therefore, if you sincerely want to work for God, how can you unite with someone trying to build his own kingdom at the expense of God's? You cannot. The "unity" would not work. It would be false.

There are those who say, "Yes, but we can fellowship together without agreeing on everything. We just will not talk about those things on which we do not agree."

Have you ever tried that? Eventually the differences create a conflict. The Word says, **Can two walk together, except they be agreed?** (Amos 3:3). You can pretend to agree with someone, but if you really do not, your disagreements — talked about or not — will affect your fellowship.

For there to be true Christian unity, these three things must be present in a relationship.

Christians certainly cannot have fellowship with those who are not part of God's family.

What fellowship has light with darkness?

2 Corinthians 6:14 NAS

Your "light" will grow dim the longer you fellowship with those in darkness. There is no way you can have real fellowship with people who are not walking in light. David found this out the hard way.

8

Say *No* to a
Wandering Mind

David is a prime example of a man who did not say *no* and later was deeply grieved because he had not. Eve could be blamed in Adam's case, but the woman in this case cannot be blamed. It was all David's fault.

First of all, as king, David should have been out leading his men in the battle, instead of staying at home.

> **And it came to pass, after the year was expired, at the time when kings go forth to battle, that David sent Joab, and his servants with him, and all Israel; and they destroyed the children of Ammon, and besieged Rabbah.** *But David tarried still at Jerusalem.*
>
> **2 Samuel 11:1**

Second, David should not have had so much idle time on his hands. He was sitting around looking for something to do. Idle time almost always means devil's time. That does not mean you have to be going ninety miles an hour, working yourself to death. It does mean that you do not sit around and let your mind wander where it will, either. David was being lazy. His mind began to wander, and then from his rooftop he saw Bathsheba bathing.

He should have yelled, "*No*, flesh! *No.*"

Instead, he sent for her to come visit him. Because David was the king, she had to obey him. He misused his authority to gratify his own flesh. That was bad enough, but unfortunately, it did not stop there. To cover his first sin, he committed another — murder. He had Bathsheba's husband killed.

That is the terrible thing about indulging the flesh. If you give in to it in small ways, before you know it, you are giving in to the flesh in greater ways.

Small Sins Lead to Bigger Sins

All David had to do was say *no*, and it would have been anointed. The small sin of saying *yes* to his eyes led to saying *yes* to his body and then *yes* to murder. Consequently, God sent his prophet Nathan to correct David.

The result, as everyone knows who has read the Old Testament, is that the child born of David and Bathsheba's sin died. Sin does not pay.

David's sin has never been forgotten. Even the world remembers it, and of course, magnifies it into deceptively glamorous situations. Today we have pornographic movies titled, *David and Bathsheba* and *Samson and Delilah*. What a way to be remembered!

The names of David and Samson have been bywords for saying *yes* to the flesh for thousands of years. If they had simply said *no*, their names today would be associated only with godly things and not with dirty movies. God's people must learn to say *no* to the flesh.

9

Say No to Your Children

Another area where people do not say *no* often enough is to their children. Many great men throughout history have lost their anointing, and sometimes, their ministries because they did not raise their children according to Biblical principles. One of those is also found in the books of Samuel.

> **Now the sons of Eli were sons of Belial** [or sons of the devil]; **they knew not the Lord.**
>
> 1 Samuel 2:12

Eli's sons knew not the Lord. Why not? Why did Eli not teach and train them up in the Lord? Why did he let them do whatever they wanted? Because he never learned to say *no* to them. Look what happened:

> **Wherefore the sin of the young men** [Eli's sons] **was very great before the Lord: for men abhorred the offering of the Lord.**
>
> **But Samuel ministered before the Lord, being a child . . . .**
>
> **Moreover his mother made him a little coat, and brought it to him from year to year, when she came up with her husband to offer the yearly sacrifice.**
>
> 1 Samuel 2:17-19

Notice, we have two kinds of people in this situation. The sons of Eli were born into his lineage of the priesthood. They were expected to be pure and upright. But they were not.

Then there was Samuel who was not born into the priesthood but brought into it. If you read 1 Samuel 2, you will see that he lived a different kind of life before the Lord than Eli did. As he was dedicated to the Lord's service and grew up in the house of the Lord under Eli, he lived a holy, pure life.

After he grew older, Samuel told Eli that his sons were using their office of priest to entice the women of Israel into illicit sex. (1 Sam. 2:22.) They also were taking portions of the animals brought for offerings that by law were not allocated to the priesthood. (vv. 13-17.)

Sin of Eli's Sons Continues

The sons of the high priest, the prophet Eli, were having sex at the door of the tabernacle! This sin still goes on today. Adultery among the ministry and in the Church is just as much an abomination to God as it was then. Sexual sins have caused more problems in Christians and in religious matters than most of us know.

What did Eli do? He said:

> **Nay, my sons; for it is no good report that I hear: ye make the Lord's people to transgress.**

> **1 Samuel 2:24**

Well, "whoop-de-doo"! He should have taken authority over the situation, whatever it took, and said a firm *no* to his sons. Instead of slapping them on their wrists and saying, "Naughty, naughty," Eli should have removed them from serving until they repented and changed their ways. His *no* should have been so loud, bold, and strong that there was no question of the consequences if they continued in their sins. Eli learned the hard way that *no* is anointed.

A man of God came to Eli with a prophecy of judgment from the Lord:

"I told you to take care of your sons. Because you did not take care of your sons, I am going to remove you and your lineage from this position." (vv. 27-36.)

Eli did not say *no* to his sons, and he lost the priesthood for his descendants and even the lives of his sons. Eli's sons caused the Lord's people to transgress, and Eli never dealt with the problem. Because he did not, he was removed along with them.

What a sad ending for Eli because he did not put his foot down and say, "*No*, my sons, you will not do these things anymore, or I will take care of you."

Hope Does Not Replace *No*

We still have the same problem today with a lot of ministries and in a lot of Christian homes. People are not saying *no* to their children. They are not saying *no* to the things of the devil designed to split their families.

People just hope everything will all work out. Hoping will not solve the problem. Not saying *no* will destroy you! It will cause you to lose everything. The Bible shows examples of this over and over!

The truly amazing thing about the story of Eli and his sons is that Samuel, who grew up seeing the situation and was even used by God to warn Eli, allowed the same problem to develop in his own family! God used him mightily to warn another man about not saying *no*, then he turned around and committed the same sin.

Samuel did not say *no* to his own children, and they did evil in the sight of the Lord. Samuel followed in Eli's footsteps and did not do a thing to stop his sons.

Of all people, Samuel knew how to use the anointed word *no*. Through watching David, Saul, and Eli, he saw first hand the consequences of saying *yes* or weak *no's*. Yet he fell into the same trap.

No is a protection from Heaven. If you will use it and let your communication be *yes* and *no* with no discussion, or "Geneva summits," you will walk in victory. Right is right, and wrong is wrong. Your words will cause you to stand on whichever way you choose.

When you say *no* to your children, mean it. They may whine and mope, but *no* gives them security. Your child may want that thirteenth cookie, but tell him, "No, you can't have another cookie."

Whine, whine, whine, and your cute little boy may reach for it again. Don't let him. Say *no*. He may not like it now, but when he grows up with standards and a sense of security, he will come home in later years and say, "Thanks, Mom and Dad."

When you go to his house, you will see his children being brought up right. You will see him saying *no* when he should. He learned it from you!

10

No in the New Testament

We have looked at several examples from the Old Testament where *no* was not used properly. However, one of the best examples of someone who should have said *no* is found in the New Testament. That man was Judas. His flesh and his greed said *yes, yes, yes,* and he ended in destruction. In Luke 22:3-6, we read:

> Then entered Satan into Judas surnamed Iscariot, being of the number of the twelve.
>
> And he went his way, and communed with the chief priests and captains, how he might betray him unto them.
>
> And they were glad, and covenanted to give him money.
>
> And he promised, and sought opportunity to betray him unto them in the absence of the multitude.

Judas could have said *no* to the greed in his soul. He could have said *no* to the chief priests who besought him. When people begin seeking you with wrong motives, stop them with a loud, bold, strong NO.

This is especially true for young ministries. A lot of ministries are murdered in their infancy by people with wrong motives. If a person wants to help you, but that person's heart is not right, you had better have the backbone to say *no*. If you do not, you will be very sorry. I learned this the hard way, and I have learned to say *no*.

No Can Protect You

No is a protection for you. It can protect the call of God on your life, your destiny, your family, and your church. *No* does not need an explanation. It just needs to be *no.*

Judas could have said, "*No.* I will not betray the King of kings."

But he did betray Him. Then Judas went out and hanged himself. Saying *yes* when he should have said *no* caused him so much guilt and shame that he took his own life. *No* would have prevented that from happening.

Contrast Judas' life and death with Peter's. Peter also betrayed Jesus. In fact, Peter denied Him three times, then ran and hid when Jesus was taken away. (Mark 14.) He was more concerned with what people thought of him and with his own safety than with his relationship with Christ. He was so concerned that he refused to take a stand for Him.

He should have declared, "Yes, I know Him."

His *yes* was a *no,* and his *no* was a *yes.* Peter really was confused. However, he did repent. Judas could have repented, but he did not. Peter repented, and it was not too late for him. Peter turned his *no* into a *no* and his *yes* into a *yes.* He became a strong man for God and was used mightily in the Lord's work. His life ended in a blaze of glory and not through suicide.

Another New Testament example where *no* was not used properly is in 2 Timothy 4:10: **For Demas hath forsaken me, having loved this present world . . . .**

Paul had been training this man, Demas. What a privilege for Demas. Can you imagine the honor of being personally trained by Paul? Demas apparently did not appreciate this honor, however, for he refused to say *no* to the desires of his flesh and to the pull of the world. To fulfill his own lust, he left the greatest revivalist that the world has ever known, this man Paul.

Think of what it must have been like to sit at Paul's feet and learn how to turn nations upside down. Demas was learning from the man who wrote half the New Testament. But he loved this present world more. His flesh screamed *yes*, and he went with that. First John 2:15-17 says:

> Love not the world, neither the things that are in the world. If any man love the world, the love of the Father is not in him.
>
> For all that is in the world, the lust of the flesh, and the lust of the eyes, and the pride of life, is not of the Father, but is of the world.
>
> And the world passeth away, and the lust thereof: but he that doeth the will of God abideth for ever.

We have to say *no* to our desires, to the flesh, to this world, and to people, circumstances, and devils. *No* is anointed.

11

No Must Be Said in Love

Many times, we think people who say *no* are just being mean. However, saying *no* at the right time and place is not mean. Sometimes, saying *yes* when you should say *no* is really being mean.

Saying *no* can be mean, but only if you say it out of your soul, out of selfish desires. You cannot say *no* with bitterness or hatred and be right. The right *no* must come by the Holy Spirit in boldness but delivered in the love of God.

God says *no*, as we saw earlier in this book. He began saying *no* in the Garden of Eden, and *no* is still a major word in His vocabulary.

God said *no* to Cain's offering. (Gen. 4:1-7.)

He said, "*No*, I will not receive your substitute offering."

And He did not. He did not back down from His *no*. God always has said *no* to sin and always will. He says *no* to wrong ideas that people have. He says *no* to anything that does not line up with His Word or His will. That is His right. He is called God for one good reason: He *is* God.

God said *no* to Satan when he attempted to take over the Kingdom.

God said, "You will not do it," and then He kicked the devil out of his position and out of power and authority. (Rev. 12:7-9.)

Satan had said in his heart, **I will exalt my throne above the stars of God** (Is. 14:13).

God did not hesitate. He did not discuss opinions or strategies or compromises with the devil, and He certainly did not call a "Geneva summit" of the spirit world.

He did not say, "Let's have a committee meeting about this, and maybe we can share equal power."

God looked at Lucifer and said, "*No*, you will not. Out you go. Who do you think you are? Is the creation trying to be greater than the Creator?"

He took action immediately with a very strong, loud, bold *no*. God did not ask Satan what he thought about the situation, either. He just declared, "Out," even though one-third of the angels fell with the devil. (It does not pay to "hang out" with the wrong crowd!)

Was God mean when He said *no* to Lucifer? Of course not. With things as bad as they are in the world because God said *no* to the devil, I would hate to think where we would all be if God had let him do whatever he wanted!

Jesus said, **I beheld Satan as lightning fall from heaven** (Luke 10:18).

When Satan fell, it was noticeable. If God says *no*, and you try to change that *no* to a *yes*, it will cause you to fall, also.

12

No Means Taking a Stand

Another important fact you need to know about the anointed word *no* is that it will create enemies at times. You might as well get prepared for that. Many people are not used to hearing *no* in today's permissive society, and they do not like it when you use it. That is why a lot of people do not use the word more often — no one likes enemies. We all like to be liked. However, I would rather say *no* and be God's friend than not say it and have a group of losers for friends, wouldn't you?

No Makes Enemies

If you want to be God's friend, you must stand on the truth and declare *no* when it should be *no*, and *yes* when it should be *yes*. The Bible says that in the last days there will be those who hate Christians for His name's sake. Say *no* sometimes, and it is a guaranteed result that you will have enemies.

Remember, however, **Greater is he that is in you, than he that is in the world** (1 John 4:4), and **No weapon that is formed against thee shall prosper** (Is. 54:17).

A missionary friend of mine is alive today because she said *no* and then stood on God's Word. Late one night in a foreign country by herself, she was surrounded by ten men. Great fear attempted to engulf her because she is blonde and fair-skinned, and she knew those men were attracted by her looks and meant her no good.

Everything inside her was screaming to run, she told me, but she knew there was no way she could outrun them all. She had to say *no* to what her soul was thinking and to the reactions of her flesh. The two scripture verses quoted above rose up in her spirit, she said.

She pointed to one of the men and said loud, bold, and strong, "*No*, no you don't! Move out of my way. In Jesus' name, get out of my way. I am coming through."

At first, the men just stood there leering at her.

Then she pointed her finger and said, "In Jesus' name, move, NOW."

One man bowed to her and motioned her past, so she walked on through the men. When she got around the corner, she ran for her life!

No protected her. She stood on the name of Jesus and on His Word and declared a strong *no*. The devil is out to destroy us, but if we rise up and boldly declare *no* to ungodly things, he cannot harm us. It is time the Church rose up and declared her position.

In these last days, many will be deceived. The Bible says that even some of "the elect" will go astray. Why? They have not learned to say *no*. Those who will not be deceived will be fought by those who are deceived.

Saying *no* to their doctrines and to their operations causes some people to become your enemies. Some will not like you, and some may hate you. When you say *no,* some may fight you tooth and nail. But do not waver. Keep saying *no, no, no.* If God be for you, who can be against you?

No **Has a Backbone**

One of the things my grandmother used to say to me is, "Any old dead fish can float down the river, but it takes one with backbone to swim up the river against the current."

No is part of our spiritual backbone. God did not make us to be spineless jellyfish. He made us in His image, and God has a backbone. It does not take a backbone to go with the flow of people's ideas, thoughts, and opinions. If they are wrong, we need to realize God made us with a backbone, and we can say *no*.

Look at all the people to whom God said *no*: Lucifer, Adam and Eve, Cain, Samson, David, Saul, Eli, Samuel, Judas. God is not afraid to use the word *no,* and we should not be either. We are made in God's image, so that means we also can say *no* at the proper time and place. Through His Word, He teaches us when and how to say *no*.

In addition to accounts of those who did not say *no* at the proper time and place, the Bible gives stories of those who did:

Noah, Abraham, Joseph, Joshua and Caleb, Daniel, and Esther of the Old Testament, and Joseph, Mary's husband, in the New Testament, as well as the disciples Peter and John, and the Apostle Paul.

41

13

No Affects Destinies

God told Noah to build an ark. Noah built it, but not without opposition. The entire time he was constructing the ark, his countrymen were making jokes at his expense and criticizing him. However, Noah said *no* to men and *yes* to God.

After he built the ark, Noah and his family climbed into it. Can you imagine the reaction from his neighbors?

"What are you doing in there, Noah? Hey, Noah, where is the rain? It is not raining yet, you crazy nut. As a matter of fact, it has never rained! What are you going to do with this ark-thing anyhow? Come on out, Noah. Nothing is going to happen."

What did Noah do? He obeyed God and said *no* to those people. It is a good thing that he did, or where would we be today? *No* affects destinies, sometimes of many people. When you say *no*, it is not just your own life at stake. Your *no* may affect hundreds or thousands of people.

An example of this kind of *no* is shown in the life of Abraham. When God told him to leave his own country, Abraham had a decision to make: to obey God or stay where he was. (Gen. 12.)

I am certain that Abraham's relatives and friends thought he was crazy. They probably let him know it, too. There was no doubt a strong pull on him to remain in the land he knew so well with all the comforts, position, and conveniences that he had. But Abraham said *no* to the flesh and to other people and *yes* to God.

Abraham also said *no* to strife with Lot. It is too bad Lot did not learn from his uncle how important that little word was. It would have saved him a lot of trouble and heartache.

Abraham's great-grandson Joseph knew this. He said *no* to the temptations of Potiphar's wife. (Gen. 39:6-10.) No doubt she was one of the most beautiful women in the country, but Joseph refused her.

No May Not Look Smart

At first, it did not look like a smart move. In the long run, however, Joseph's *no* saved many lives, not just the lives of the Israelites but the lives of many Egyptians who would have starved during the famine that came later.

Your *no* also may affect many lives.

Look at Joshua and Caleb, as reported in Numbers 13 and 14. The other ten spies sent into Israel to report on the land brought back an evil report. Joshua and Caleb stood up and said *no* to the evil report and the taunts of the people. But notice who went in to possess the land. Those who said *yes* to their flesh and to fears and doubts never saw the promised land.

If we say *yes* to the devil's crowd, we will never enter into the promises and victories that are ours.

Another example of someone who said *no* was Daniel. He said *no* to the king's edict not to pray in any other name but the king's. However, Daniel obeyed

God. He opened his windows, and prayed so that everyone could hear him. (Dan. 6:10.)

Daniel was not afraid to say *no*, and the entire kingdom was turned around because Daniel did what was right in the sight of God. That took a backbone of steel. He knew the consequence would be the lion's den, but he still said *no*.

Daniel's fellow countrymen, Shadrach, Meshach, and Abednego also said *no* to the king of Babylon. (Dan. 3.) They refused to bow down and worship false idols. Their *no* was unshakeable. The king said he would throw them in the fiery furnace if they continued to say *no*. They did not waver or budge an inch. *No, no, no*, they replied.

The king threw them in the fiery furnace just as he said he would, and the three young men were engulfed by the flames. Then one of the greatest miracles ever reported took place. In front of everyone's eyes, a Fourth Man appeared in the flames!

Say *No* to the Devil

Say *no* to the devil and his crowd, and you will see miracles, also. However, you will not see miracles happening in an atmosphere that is not right. If God says *no*, and man says *yes*, you had better agree with God.

Esther and her kinsman Mordecai are two more examples of those who stood up and said *no* in the face of tremendous opposition.

Esther said *no* to her husband, the king, knowing it might cost her life. (The Book of Esther.) King

Ahasuerus honored the man named Haman and his plot to destroy the Jews. But Mordecai said *no* and would not kneel down to Haman or pay him honor. (Esth. 3:2.)

Mordecai persuaded Esther also to say *no*, and the Jewish people of that day were saved. You can be sure all of those people were glad Mordecai and Esther stood up for God and said *no* to man.

In the New Testament, Joseph is a man who affected the destinies of multitudes of people by saying *no*. In that day, if a woman became pregnant before marriage, she was liable to be stoned.

When Joseph found that Mary was pregnant and knew he was not the father, he had every right to turn her over to the authorities. But he did not. He said *no* to cultural and religious tradition and said *yes* to God. (Matt. 1:18-25.) What if Joseph had not said *no* to men and *yes* to God?

Time and time again throughout both the Old and New Testaments, we can see the results that a good, strong, bold, powerful *no* can produce.

King Herod ordered the Magi to go to Bethlehem, locate the baby, and then report back to him in Jerusalem. The Magi went to Bethlehem, but that is as far as their *yes* went. They said *no* to King Herod, and although they knew exactly where Jesus was, they never did report back to Herod. (Matt. 2:12.)

Many of the miracles in the New Testament would not have happened if people had not said *no*.

Mary Magdalene said *no* to the jeers and leers of those who said she should not go near Jesus. But she said *no* to people and *yes* to God and was totally set free. She became one of Jesus' most faithful followers.

Say *No* to Tradition

Then there was the woman with the issue of blood. She should never have been out in public. She had been hemorrhaging for twelve years. During that time, she must have been kept separate from the people because it was against the statutes of Israel to be among people if you were bleeding. Blood meant that you were unclean.

This woman knew that to go out in public and try to get to Jesus meant certain stoning and death. She did not care anymore what people thought of her.

She said *no* to people's opinion and to tradition and did everything she could to get to Jesus to receive her miracle. Her *no* to the world brought her into contact with Jesus, and she was totally healed.

Another woman who said *no* said it to Jesus! She had come to Him on behalf of her daughter who was demon possessed. (Matt. 15:22-28.) Jesus told her that He was only sent to the lost sheep of Israel and that it was not right to take the children's bread and toss it to the dogs.

The woman could have hung her head and crawled away, but she did not. She said *no* to the traditional religious barriers involved and stood up for her miracle. Jesus respected her faith and freed her daughter from bondage.

Peter and John knew the value of *no*. In Acts 4, the religious leaders commanded them not to preach Christ any longer.

But the apostles said, "*No*. We must obey God rather than you."

Then they went out and did exactly what they had been told by man not to do. Mighty miracles occurred in their ministries. Notice what they said:

> And now, Lord, behold their threatenings: and grant unto thy servants, that with all boldness they may speak thy word,
>
> By stretching forth thine hand to heal; and that signs and wonders may be done by the name of thy holy child Jesus.
>
> And when they had prayed, the place was shaken where they were assembled together; and they were all filled with the Holy Ghost, and they spake the word of God with boldness.
>
> **Acts 4:29-31**

Right after this, the story is told of two people who lied to Peter in the presence of the Holy Spirit and dropped dead. Ananias and Sapphira said *yes* to the world and lost everything. (Acts 5.)

From then on, Peter and John went out boldly performing miracles. They knew how to say *no* to man and *yes* to God.

Paul Said *No* Many Times

Another man in the Bible who seemed to love the word *no* was Paul.

When political or religious leaders tried to keep him from preaching, he said *no*. He was thrown into prison, beaten, robbed, and left for dead at various times. He could easily have decided the ministry was too tough and quit. But he did not.

Paul said:

I am not ashamed of the gospel of Christ (Rom:1:16), and **for me to live is Christ, and to die is gain** (Phil. 1:21).

There were probably plenty of opportunities for Paul to give up and go on to be with the Lord.

But he said, "*No*, I will press on," and he did.

Paul was never one to mince words. His *yes* was yes, and his *no* was no. He may have had few close friends, but he certainly was God's close friend. Why? Paul knew when to say *yes* and when to say *no*.

Half the New Testament was written by Paul. If you read his epistles very closely, you will find *no* in them over and over again. He knew the importance of saying *no*.

If Paul were alive today, he would more than likely look us in the eye and exclaim, *"Just say no!"*

14

When To Say *No*

There are a number of things in the Word to which God has told us to say *no*. Among these are: devils, certain brothers in the Lord, evil, torment of the past, certain women, fools, and liars.

He said to have no fellowship with devils. (1 Cor. 10:20.) How do you have fellowship with the devil? By accepting demons and allowing them to have influence in your life. *No* means absolutely no acceptance of that thing, that person, or that particular idea. *No* stops things from coming into existence in your life.

In 1 Corinthians 5:11, the Word warns us not even to eat with certain brothers.

> **But now I have written unto you not to keep company, if any man that is called a brother be a fornicator, or covetous, or an idolator, or a railer, or a drunkard, or an extortioner; with such an one *no* not to eat.**

The Bible does not mince words here. Paul wrote very clearly not to even eat with these people. That does not mean to go over and try to save them. Yes, there are some cases where you may help someone, but in other cases, the Word is very explicit. *Just say no.*

Paul is not even talking about sinners here, but a brother. He is very explicit: Don't even eat with them!

Why is he so emphatic? He did not intend for the Corinthians to misunderstand him. If we get around people like that, the world begins to pull on us as well as them. God wants us to say *no* to any fellowship with the devil.

People say, "But it is not flesh and blood against which we war. It is principalities, powers, and wickedness in high places." (Eph. 6:12; 2 Cor. 10:3-5.)

Love the Person, Not Their Sin

That is true. But guess who the wickedness comes through? People, so we need to avoid such people. You can continue to love the person in the name of Jesus, but if they do not change, you have to say *no* to them. Otherwise, you will be allowing whatever is in them to jump onto you, your family, your church, and so forth. Say *no* to whatever their sin is, and save your time and energy fighting it off.

The Bible says, **Abhor that which is evil; cleave to that which is good** (Rom. 12:9), or "Say *no* to that which is evil, and say *yes* to that which is good."

If you are going to love God, you must learn to hate evil with a passion. You must campaign against the evil of this world. Campaign in prayer. Protest personally against the works of the devil.

The Bible also says, **Resist the devil, and he will flee from you** (James 4:7). What does it mean *to resist*? It means to say *no*. Say, "*No*, devil," and he has to go roam somewhere else, because *no* shuts every door and window, and pulls down the blinds so the devil cannot even see inside. *No* is a glorious word that keeps the devil out.

Say *No* to the Devil's Reminders

No shuts the door to the torment of being haunted by your past. At times, demons will take the past and try to torment, or haunt, us with it — especially if we have not asked forgiveness for something. Unforgiveness really opens the door to the devil's tricks. That is why it is so important to walk in love and to repent immediately when we do something we should not.

The devil loves to remind you of past mistakes. In fact, he seems to deal more with the past than with anything else. If God has forgiven us and erased those sins or mistakes, then we need to leave them erased. Say *no* to the devil's haunting, and he has to flee. He will run from you, if you say *no*. Keep saying *no* until he quits harassing and haunting you with that thing. Find a verse on which to stand. *No* is like a razor. It sets you free.

Proverbs talks a lot about saying *no*. One proverb tells men to stay away from those women who "cry out in the streets" for you to come into their beds. The Word did not say for us to interview them to find out why they do what they do, or to take pictures and write articles and books about them.

I know one person who had a "street ministry to prostitutes and homosexuals." The next thing I knew — he was both! I know that is a wild statement, but it is the truth. The Word does not tell us to interview such people and get on their level in order "to relate better" to them. The Word says to tell them the good news, then go.

The Word also says, "Tell fools *no.*" Proverbs 23:9 says that if you talk with a fool, he will despise the wisdom of your words. The only way you can deal with some people is just to say *no* and walk on without turning back.

Also, Proverbs 19:22 says *no* to liars. Say, "*No.* I am not going to walk with you. You are a liar. Goodby."

No is powerful. *No* will protect you. So why do people not use it more? For several reasons, but usually because they do not understand what *no* is.

15

Reasons Why People Do Not Say *No*

The first reason *no* is not used much anymore is that people are no longer accustomed to absolutes. As a proclaimer of the word *no*, you stand alone. In the world today, if *no* is said, it almost always is given with an excuse. It is not the absolute that it should be.

The soul does not like *no* and *yes*. They are "commitment" words. People are afraid of that today.

No is contagious. If it is used correctly, it will be a healthy contagiousness. What the Church needs today is a *no* epidemic. We would be a lot healthier.

The world says, "Whatever you want, it's okay. If it feels good, do it. Whatever makes you happy."

We do not need that philosophy from the pit of hell in the Church.

The second reason *no* is not popular is that it causes reactions.

People do not always receive *no* in a nice way nor with the acceptance we all crave. The primary reason people do not like to say *no* is because the reactions they often get are hard to cope with.

Many times, people will ask you, "Why?" But remember that *no* is an anointed word that does not need to be explained. In fact, most of the time, it should not be explained. By explaining, many times you may lose the force of the declaration.

My grandmother, who helped with my upbringing, always said, "When I say *no*, it is *no* forever."

There was no changing her mind, and that is the way it should be in the realm of the spirit. Somehow, today, our *no* means very little. It has been so watered down. Most of the time, it turns into a social *yes*, or a soulish *yes*. Either one will get you in big trouble.

No Angers Rebellious People

No angers dominant or controlling people, or those with self-will and rebellion. Watch for their reactions. People will come up with all sorts of excuses, reasons, and explanations to counteract your *no*. They will cry or get mad and yell. They will try all sorts of things to move you off your stand. Emotional manipulation comes into full manifestation when you start saying *no* to people who do not like the sound of that word.

One reaction to *no* is self-pity. I like helping poor people, but I refuse to help lazy people. You are not helping someone if you help them to "mooch." The Bible says that if you do not work, you are not to eat. (2 Thess. 3:10.) And the Word says if you do not feed your family, you are worse than an infidel. (1 Tim. 5:8.) That is a heavy statement, but it is true. I did not make it up. The Bible states it.

Watch out for professional beggars who make the church rounds. When you recognize them and say *no*, they may cry and begin emotional manipulation plays. If you are not careful, you will change your *no* to a *yes*.

Self-pity is a common reaction to *no*. Self-pity always pleases the flesh of a person.

A third reason people do not say *no* is guilt.

Often, people feel guilty at saying *no*, as if it were a dirty word or a bad word. It is so rarely used today, it sounds funny to our ears.

I have learned to say *no* to people and go on about my business, not even thinking of the incident again. You have to learn to say *no* and walk away. You should not feel any guilt by saying *no* when it should be said.

Do Not Hesitate To Say *No*

People motivated by mercy can be abused more than others because they find it so hard to say *no*. However, of all people, they need to learn to say it, go home, and not feel guilty. People will run you ragged, if you do not stop them. Demons will run you crazy, if you do not stop them.

Suppose a friend calls with free tickets to a basketball game an afternoon when the Lord has called you to pray. You find it so difficult to say *no* that you say, "Well, let me think about it." You know you should not go, but you waver and then give in and go. The next day you feel rotten because you know you should not have gone.

Even if you get the courage to call and cancel your plans, you feel guilty. What should have been a strong, positive *no* turned into a puny, miserable, guilty *no*. If you had said *no* in the first place, there would have been no guilt. All of us have fallen into this trap at one time or another.

A fourth reason why people do not say *no* more often is because they think it sounds mean. It sometimes sounds mean because the soul does not like to be told *no*. The soul likes its own way.

If your child squirms away from you and runs toward the street where traffic is rushing by, you scream, "No!"

Was that mean? Of course not. That *no* was the nicest thing you could say. It was protection for your child.

Suppose you have just gotten up in the morning and are beginning to pray. Your soul and body are saying, "Sleep, sleep. We need more sleep." They do not need more sleep. Say, "*No*, we are going to pray, so shut up." Is it mean to tell your body and soul *no* when your spirit knows it is far better to be praying? No, it is not mean but good.

I say *no* a lot. I know *no* is not mean, but not everyone else does yet. A lot of people call and want me to preach in their churches. I pray over the invitations I get. If God wants me to go, I say *yes*. If God tells me not to go, I say *no*.

A Personal Example

I have discovered that some people will not take *no* for an answer. They keep trying to get you to change your mind.

"But, Brother Liardon, you have to come to these meetings. They just will not be successful unless you come," they tell me.

I reply, "That is the problem. You do not want me or the gift of the Holy Spirit operating through me. You want to draw people. If the meeting will not be successful without my presence, it is not God. I am not coming. Thank you for asking me, but *no*, I am not coming. Goodby."

I will not hold meetings to help someone "draw crowds." I only go when the Lord says to go and when He has something He wants said to those people. That should be the only reason for anyone to have a meeting.

The people may say, "Please, Brother Liardon. We will guarantee you all this money."

But I still say *no*. My answer is *no* forever unless God tells me otherwise. Money cannot buy me.

A certain pastor who had a tendency to be "pushy" called my office one time and hassled one of the men who works for me. He wanted this staff member to give him my phone number so that he could discuss my holding a meeting for him.

My worker replied, "He is out on a trip right now. If you will give us your name and number, we will pass it on to him, and he will get back to you."

The pastor persisted, "Well, where is he? I will call him myself."

Our ministry policy does not permit that, and my staff knows it.

My staff member said, "We don't like to disturb him during a meeting. We'll call him and give him your name and number. Then he will call you when he can. Otherwise, you can call him when he returns."

Then this pastor yelled at the man who works for me. He not only yelled, but he also swore at him. The man who works for me has wisdom. He did not yell back. He did not even tell me what had happened until some time later.

But one day we were looking over our invitations, praying about them, and working out a schedule for the future. We came to this pastor's invitation, and I asked my staff member about it. He still did not tell me what happened, but his voice was not right. I know my people and I know their voices. (You need to know your family like that. You can help them in time of trouble and they can help you.)

I said, "Your voice does not sound right. What is the problem here?"

Then he told me what this pastor had done.

"Lose his phone number forever!" I instructed my worker.

Eventually, that pastor called again and started the whole routine, "You must come to our church. You are such a gift to the Body . . . ."

I said, "Sir, would you be quiet for a moment? I want to talk to you, and I want you to know why I am doing what I am doing. I don't want any confusion here. I want you to understand me clearly.

"First of all, I am glad you called. I am glad you like my ministry and that you have read my books. That is very nice.

"But *I will not preach in your church*. Not now, not ever — unless God specifically tells me otherwise. You have treated one of the people who works for me badly. You even cursed him. When you do something like that to one of my people, you have done it to me. And when you have done it to them or to me, you have done it to Jesus."

He began to sputter, whine, and try to explain away his actions.

But I said, "My answer to your invitation is *no*, unless God hits me on the side of the head and tells me to go to your church. You can call. You can fuss. You can criticize. You can backbite me or stab me in the back all you want, but my answer is still *no*.

"Let me say again, however, that I want you to know why I am taking this stand. You are supposed to be a man of God. You are older than I, and I think someone who has been in the ministry as long as you have would have enough self-control not to curse."

He apologized but that did not change my *no*.

16

Five *No* Facts

1. *No* is one of the words people most wish they had said in past situations.

A young lady who graduated from high school with me is an example. A good friend of mine, she is now in her early twenties, divorced, and a mother. All because she did not say *no* one night to her boyfriend.

People are pastoring wrong churches because they did not say *no*.

Some Christians have lost their rewards or crowns in Heaven because they did not say *no* at the right time.

2. *No* originated in Heaven with God.

No and *yes* are appropriate responses to right and wrong. God originated these responses.

3. *No* protects you and stops the devil.

No would have protected the young lady I mentioned above and her entire life would have been different.

4. *No* is part of the teachings of the Bible.

We have already discussed a number of people from the Bible who said *no* when they should have said *yes*, or vice versa. The consequences of their actions are plainly written out for all who will read them to profit by.

5. *No* can be said by anyone.

You do not have to be fifty years old in the Lord before you can say *no*. You can be five seconds old in Jesus and say *no*. Anyone can say *no*.

Learning to say no is so important to our destinies.

When God says *no*, it is anointed.

Just say, ''No.''

OTHER BOOKS BY ROBERTS LIARDON

Kathryn Kuhlman
A Spiritual Biography
of God's Miracle Working Power

Spiritual Timing

Run to the Battle

I Saw Heaven

A Call to Action

The Quest for Spiritual Hunger

The Price of Spiritual Power

Breaking Controlling Powers

Religious Politics

Cry of the Spirit

VIDEOS BY ROBERTS LIARDON

Confronting Brazen Heaven

I Saw Heaven

Roar of the '90s

God's Generals

Reformers and Revivalists Series

**Available from your local bookstore
or by writing:**

Harrison House • P. O. Box 35035 • Tulsa, OK 74153

In Canada contact:

Word Alive • P. O. Box 284
Niverville, Manitoba • CANADA ROA 1EO

For international sales in Europe, contact:

Harrison House Europe • Belruptstrasse 42 A
A — 6900 Bregenz • AUSTRIA

To contact Roberts Liardon, write:

P. O. Box 30710 • Laguna Hills, CA 92654
714-661-8606